AN ILLUSTRATED INTRODUCTION TO THE
MARTIAL ARTS

Marshall Cavendish

Published by Marshall Cavendish Books Limited
58 Old Compton Street
London W1V 5PA

© Marshall Cavendish Limited 1969
This printing 1986

ISBN 0 85685 145 0

Printed and bound in Hong Kong
by Dai Nippon Printing Company

Introduction

Aikido, karate, kendo, judo . . . the very names of these oriental martial arts conjure up visions of invincible power, secret skills and a mystic philosophy. But how are these powers acquired? What is the secret of their skills and what is their history? These are the questions that this book is designed to answer.

Each section is devoted to one martial art and gives an outline of its history. The principles underlying the art concerned are clearly set out. With the help of colour photographs experienced practitioners illustrate the techniques they employ and in the text the words used to describe the actions are explained. Having read this book you should be capable of joining a martial arts class confident in the knowledge that you have a basic understanding of what is entailed in a course of training and that the terms are not foreign to you.

Warning. The sports described in these pages are derived from techniques originally developed for use in armed and unarmed combat. They can be dangerous. If you use the martial arts irresponsibly you could injure yourself as well as someone else. Never use your skills against anyone other than a willing fellow practitioner. Ideally you should practise only under the supervision of a skilled instructor in a proper training session.

Contents

Karate-1

Karate is the ultimate art of unarmed combat as well as being a superb system of achieving physical fitness and control. It provides an unequalled form of gaining supreme control of the body and a sharp discipline of mind. Although it involves many hours of practice, karate will provide you with the means to health, suppleness, speed and agility of mind.

Karate simultaneously develops all the powers of your body and your mind. It strengthens and trains your hands, head, knees, feet and elbows so that they can be used as powerful weapons, capable of delivering effective blows in situations in which you need to defend yourself. Your entire body will be more alert and able to perform with style and accomplishment. And karate gives you such control and presence of mind that you will be able to handle most problems with which you are confronted.

This method of improving the body and the mind is found in the actual training system of karate which concentrates on the optimum use of principles taught in physics and physiology. The body's movements are perfectly harmonized in techniques involving subtle balance and controlled strength. The mind is mastered through meditation techniques and is expressed in self-confidence and self-awareness.

The role of karate in modern life is multiple. It is highly praised as an art form and, as a system of self-defence, it is widely taught in private clubs, law enforcement agencies and colleges. It is, however, the sporting aspect of karate that is responsible for the tremendous surge of popularity that it enjoys throughout the world. As an exciting, challenging and competitive sport karate has few equals.

There are numerous karate styles and techniques. In a series of five illustrated articles you will learn the Shotokan approach which originated on the island of Okinawa, lying midway between China and Japan, and now enjoys enormous popularity throughout Europe and the United States. Once you have attained a certain level of proficiency, however, it does not matter which karate technique you started with. You will then be able to absorb other styles.

The once popular but erroneous image of karate as a mysterious, brick breaking, killer art is gradually being erased. In its place the true essence and philosophy of the art has been brought to light. As such karate is being seen as a most advanced means of combating day-to-day stress and perfecting physical fitness.

Resolve to start learning karate and you will gain a life-long boon to your health and general well-being. Karate offers you confidence.

ROUNDHOUSE KICK
(Mawashi geri)

The picture on the left shows one of the most effective karate kicks. Many more kicks will be shown during the five-part series. As a preparation practise the roundhouse kick. Stand with your feet apart and one foot in front of the other. The leading foot should be bent at the knee. The hand over the leading foot should be outstretched. Swing your trailing foot up and around as if you intended kicking an attacker's neck.

KARATE BASICS

To attain proficiency in karate you must first practise basic techniques. Each movement must be repeated thousands of times until your body reacts without thought when performing punching (tsuki), striking (uchi), kicking (keri) and blocking (uke) techniques. Before you start to learn karate basics in the next part of the series, practise this punch as often as you can. Stand with your left leg in front of the right. Relax. Then suddenly strike outwards ending your punch in the position shown by the model.

SPARRING (Kumite)

What should you wear when practising karate? The traditional dress is known as a gi and consists of a loose pair of trousers and a double breasted top held closed by a belt.

A person just beginning to learn karate wears a white belt. As you become more skilled at karate you are graded with a different coloured belt. These start with the white belt then progress to the yellow, green, purple, brown and black belts. You can buy all of this clothing —except the black belt—at most sports shops. Karate clubs also supply clothing.

After diligent practice of the karate basics you must then learn the principles of sparring. Using each of the basic techniques you will learn to attack an opponent and block attacks made against you.

You will advance in training by learning various ways of applying the basics until you are ready to participate in free-style sparring.

All blows in sparring must be stopped just short of contact to ensure that serious injuries do not happen. One of the tests of proficiency in karate is the ability to focus even the strongest techniques just short of the target.

Sparring requires great concentra-tion and the ability to anticipate an opponent's movements. To be able to do this with any degree of success requires intense mental training lasting over a long period of time. This is perhaps one of the most difficult aspects of karate to master. A section of the five-part series on karate will show you how to ap-proach mental training, explaining some of the meditation techniques which you can use.

The above pictures show two op-ponents sparring. The model on the right attacks with a kick. The model on the left is blocking this kick with his left hand while prepar-ing to counter-attack with a right hand punch to the stomach. Try this with a fellow practitioner.

Free sparring is one of the most exciting parts of karate technique. It involves lightning reactions, total concentration and the ability to move with tremendous speed and economy of style. Free sparring is the best opportunity which a karate student has to practise his techniques in as near to life situations as possible, without causing any bodily harm.

When practised by very advanced karate students, free sparring displays all the grace and controlled athleticism of the ancient samurai sword fights. They move with amazing speed and agility and yet with a discipline of mind which takes many years to acquire.

Free sparring is the application of all the basic techniques of karate. After practising these techniques for many thousands of repetitions you will be ready to try them in a free sparring contest.

A free sparring competition requires great care and control so that nobody is hurt. It is wise to do it under the supervision of a Sensei (a karate master). This ensures a high safety factor.

Before you start the free sparring part of the course it is therefore advisable to join a club. In this way you can learn more quickly as well as gaining from the enthusiasm and knowledge of other karate students. There are many clubs in most cities throughout the world and you should have no difficulty in joining.

Karate can be practised by both men and women. At first, there is no reason that women should not progress as quickly as men in learning basic techniques. However, when they become fairly proficient and start free sparring they will be at an obvious disadvantage in that they are not as strong as most men.

This has not discouraged many female enthusiasts who have developed other aspects of their technique to overcome this. Most karate clubs train male and female students at the same time.

KATA

The formal exercises in karate are known as kata. These are numerous and consist of a series of techniques performed in sequence. They include all the various hand, feet and body shifting techniques used in kicking, punching, striking and blocking.

Katas were devised by the ancient karate masters and have been handed down over many years. They still form a substantial part of the karate student's training.

When you start to learn karate you will have to devote a large part of your training time to practising katas. This series will only teach you the basic katas. To learn the more complicated ones you can join a karate club. As a preparation for the karate basics practise the part of one of the katas shown in the picture on the right.

Below. A desire for an effective means of self-defence is probably one of the main reasons for the tremendous growth of karate throughout the world. It must be emphasized, however, that karate is not magical and does not render you immune to danger.

Karate-2

Karate requires discipline, alertness and dedication from the student who is learning its techniques. These qualities are particularly important while you are acquiring the skills of basic movements. To master the basic techniques of karate you must be prepared to practise consistently and with patience. Remember that you are laying the foundations for one of the most sophisticated, graceful and powerful martial arts which has been adopted from the Orient.

The basic training of karate can be broken down into various techniques such as stances (dachi), blocking (uke), punching (tsuki) and kicking (keri). There are a great number of movements in each of these categories, demanding diligence and control from the student who sets about mastering them. This, the second of the karate course presents just a few of the basic techniques for you to practise before proceeding to a deeper study of fighting and defence skills.

Each technique is divided into separate movements which must be repeated time and time again. On gaining familiarity with these movements you can learn to apply them with ever increasing speed and strength. Posture and balance are an important part of these movements.

When you are on the way to mastering basic techniques you will also learn how to practise them in different combinations so that you can move from stance to stance controlling your balance and simultaneously delivering a vast array of blocking, punching, kicking and striking techniques with immense speed.

While learning the basic techniques of karate you must apply the maximum amount of speed, strength and force to each movement every time you repeat it. You must learn which set of muscles to use to gain optimum results from each technique. The idea of a karate blow is similar to a whiplash. Force is generated from the handle of the whip (stance and hips) and travels through the length of the whip (the body) until it reaches the striking area (clenched fist or ball of the foot). Maximum power is unleased at the point of impact. In techniques such as the reverse punch, for example, you must learn to focus your entire strength on the point of impact by twisting your hips, snapping your shoulder muscles straight and slamming forth your arms and fist while simultaneously tensing your legs, hips, stomach and back muscles for a fraction of time before recoiling like a tightly wound up spring.

To do this effectively requires a great deal of controlled speed and applied strength which can only be learned in dedicated practice. Karate will teach you a whole new way of living with more mental and physical control.

STANCE (Dachi)

There are many different stances in karate, each one designed to be used in varying conditions of training and actual combat. These stances form the base from which all other techniques are developed. No matter how strong a punch or block the force will be lost before the point of contact if the foundation of the movement is weak. Through hard and constant training, however, you can develop one of the first essentials for good karate—a strong stance. When you are learning karate it is a good idea to develop one particular stance as fully as you possibly can rather than trying to master a variety of stances over a long period of time.

Try to perfect the stance shown above. It is called the back stance (kokutsu-dachi) and it is a basic stance which is used to begin many karate techniques.

Place yourself in the position of the model in the picture. Your right leg is roughly at 45 degrees to a line drawn directly forward. Bend your rear leg and place most of your weight over it.

Clench your fists and place your arms in alignment with your thighs. The back stance is an effective base from which to block attack or initiate punches and kicks in defence. Learn to be able to tense and relax your body at will. This requires great control.

BLOCKING (Uke)

Karate is a system of defence and not a means to effective but needless aggression. The primary aim of any person practising karate is to defend himself, friends or any powerless people against acts of aggression—but only if there is no other alternative open to him.

Karate blocks are an excellent means of defence. There are a wide variety of such blocks, and they take time and practice to master.

Start by learning the upper block (jodan-age-uke) shown above. This will enable you to fend off attacks to your head and neck.

Stand in the position of the model in the picture on the far left. Keep your legs together and your knees slightly bent. Raise your left hand to eye level, palm open. Your right hand should be clenched in a fist and held by your side.

Step forward with your right leg as shown in the centre picture. At the same time, begin to bring your right fist upwards across your chest, finally ending the block as shown in the picture on the right. Your left arm should now be held behind your back.

Each step of the block must be made as quickly as possible. But each step must be correct. Competency should not be sacrificed for speed. Practise slowly at first and gradually speed up your movements as you become better. Tense your body at the moment of imaginary impact and keep your muscles taut only for a fraction of a second. Then relax. This kind of control is important if you wish to be successful at karate.

UPPER BLOCK (Application)

The above picture shows a practical demonstration of the upper block being used against an opponent. The attacker on the left has tried to attack with a punch. The defender has blocked his attack using the upper block and the back stance. Notice that the defender has not only blocked the punch but also moved the attacker's arm outwards so that it cannot be used for defence when he counterattacks with an effective and strong punch.

With the tremendous growth of karate throughout the world, there are ample bone fide clubs in which you can study the art of karate.

It is of the utmost importance, however, that you check the credentials of the instructor and club teaching methods, and to which organization it is affiliated in order to establish a good future pattern of development in karate. Once a wrong technique is practised at the outset and you acquire moderate skill in its execution, you will find it very difficult to improve further and to re-learn the correct way.

Most countries have a Karate Union, supervising national activities. It is a good idea to check with such a federation about the club you are thinking of joining. In this way you can avoid a mistake.

PUNCHING (Tsuki)

There are many karate punches, each very effective when carried out correctly. The application of punching techniques enables the person who is learning karate to deliver devastating blows. The effectiveness of such punches have been shown by masters who have demonstrated the ability to break brick or thick pieces of wood. This requires many years of practice, however, and should not be tried by a student.

STEPPING PUNCH (Oi-zuki-chudan)

Stand in the position of the model in the top left picture. Keep both feet firmly on the ground. Stretch out your left arm and clench both your fists.

Then begin the punch by starting to move your right arm and leg forwards, the right leg brushing against the left leg and your right fist passing against your waist as shown in the top right picture.

Continue to move your right leg and arm forwards as shown in the bottom left picture.

The bottom right picture shows the final delivery of the stepping punch as it makes impact.

You must be relaxed while going through these movements. At the same time, the punch must be performed in a fast, flowing motion culminating in a tightening of the muscles when the punch is effected. Do not move out of your stance or over-reach forward. You may lose your balance and be put into an immediate position of vulnerability.

REVERSE PUNCH (Gyaku zuki)

This punch is similar to the stepping punch except that the blow is struck with the opposite hand to the leading foot.

The reverse punch is the most commonly used blow in karate competition since it can be delivered quickly after blocking an opponent's attack. Stand in the position of the model in the top insert picture. Stretch out your right arm and bend your right knee slightly. Your left hand should be held close to the top of the hips.

Without moving the stance of your legs, begin to reverse the positions of your hands, keeping the left fist clenched, as shown in the lower insert picture.

The punch is made in the position shown in the large picture. Notice that the feet are still in the same position. But the direction of the hips has changed to add extra force to the punch.

Practise this punch using a flowing motion but remember to relax the body until you punch.

It is unwise to extend your arms when practising any of the karate punches. This is bad for the joints of your body. Adopt the habit of holding back the striking arm, never using the full impact effect of which you are capable.

In a competition or real life situation, the philosophy of karate punching is based on the idea that one really effective punch is better than a series of weak blows. So each punch should be carried out with great concentration and power, and with an equal amount of control.

KICKING (Keri)

The application of kicking techniques differs from most other forms of martial combat. The ability to deliver a kick to the groin, knee, foot, stomach or head gives most karate proponents a decided advantage over practitioners of other attack and defence systems.

A karate master's most devastating attacks come from his feet, the power of a karate kick being more powerful than a punch. Use extreme caution when practising.

FRONT KICK (Mae-geri)

The above picture shows a powerful front kick being used against an opponent's throat and chin. This is one of the simplest yet most effective karate kicks.

Try it for yourself. Stand in the position of the model in the top left picture, keeping both your fists clenched and your left knee slightly bent.

Now raise your right knee as far as you can as shown in the top right picture. This is an important part of the kick.

Then snap your foot forward from the knee as depicted in the bottom left illustration.

Practise this kick using a fairly fast, flowing movement.

When practising the front kick, it is important to lift the knee as high as possible before thrusting outwards. The blow should be effected by the side edge of the foot or the heel. The leg should be tensed at the moment of impact.

It is important to develop steady balance when practising.

HOW TO PLAY

Grading All schools of karate have a different method of grading. But they are all based on the judo principles of Kyu (pupil) and Dan (degree) grades. The lower levels are judged more on the precision of their techniques than on fighting ability, but as a student advances he has to take part in free-sparring.

Kumite (sparring) As a karate blow can be extremely dangerous, punches and kicks have to be 'pulled' in contests. The object is to pierce an opponent's guard, and before hitting him withdraw the blow. A match is adjudicated by a referee and four judges, one judge sitting in each corner of the 9-metre-square contest area. If a judge sees an ippon (point) or waza-ari (almost a point) he blows a whistle and shows with a flag who he thinks has scored. If the referee agrees, he declares the point. Just one point – which in real life might have been a fatal or a disabling blow – is needed for victory.

Kata (forms) Contests are also held in kata – a series of regularized movements where competitors are marked on the precision of their movements and correct posture. The preliminary rounds are conducted on a knock-out basis. In the final pool, seven judges officiate with numbered cards. The highest and lowest scores are discarded and the remaining five aggregated.

The individual with the highest score is the winner.

Training All styles of karate are based on hard and regular training. There are three main training methods: basic techniques, kata, and kumite, and sessions usually last a minimum of one hour. Some styles, notably shotakan, restrict jiyu-kumite (free sparring) until the 3rd Kyu is reached, usually after two year's hard training. This is because the less experienced karateka lacks control, and can also ruin his style by sparring too early. Basic techniques, including combinations of kicks and punches, are repeated time and again in a bid to reach perfection, while kata helps to brush up the basic movements.

Karate-3

Free sparring is one of the most attractive and colourful aspects of karate. It displays disciplined agility, controlled speed and the effortless flow of two opponents using their bodies in an educated and graceful way. To learn its subtleties is to master the techniques of karate. It will enable you to use them in a spontaneous display of speed, strength and force.

Although a new karate student does not engage in free sparring (Jiyu kumite) at the outset of his training, he will at once practice the application of all the various techniques he has learned through his basic training. Simple one-step attacks and blocks, such as a stepping punch to the face (oi zuki jodan) being blocked by a rising block (age uke), are the beginnings of learning to free spar. The student then progresses to three-step attack sparring by moving forward while his opponent moves backward, countering the third block with a reverse punch to the stomach (gyaku-zuki). Then follows five-step attack sparring (Gohon Kumite) which is simply an addition of two more movements. These must be practised with as many students as possible to help build up confidence and ability, and to

prepare each student for more advanced sparring training.

The next stage in training is to vary the attacks and counters under the guidance of a teacher until the student is ready to apply techniques on his own in semi-free one attack sparring (Jiyu Ippon Kumite).

Finally, the student is ready to learn free style sparring (Jiyu Kumite), one of the most advanced aspects of karate. In many respects it resembles sparring in boxing except that each attack is stopped just short of contact with the opponent. The reason for this is the obvious danger of serious injury if a vital part of the body is hit with a strongly focussed attack. One of the tests of proficiency for an advanced student in karate is to focus even the most powerful techniques just short of target.

The free style attitude in karate is one of watchful but relaxed preparedness. Each opponent weighs the other up looking for openings to strike while at the same time being prepared to block an oncoming blow and counterattack with another. Actual sparring consists of a free exchange of blows, blocks and counterattacks until one opponent gets in a focussed attack.

It is at this point in training that the major sporting attraction of Karate comes into its own. There are many local competitions and regional championships in most parts of the world in which a student can enter to gain valuable knowledge and experience as well as giving him an opportunity to try his techniques against other students. A points system will decide who is the winner.

To learn the techniques of free sparring you must practise under the guidance of a karate master (Sensei). To do this you will have to join a club. Because of the widespread popularity of karate you should have no difficulties in joining a karate club (dojo).

Meanwhile you can practice some of the techniques of free sparring included in this lesson of the karate series. Exercise great caution if you are practising with a friend. Take the techniques slowly and with deliberation. In this way you will avoid injury.

The benefits you can gain from karate are in ratio to the amount of dedication and effort you put into training. Endeavour will be rewarded with agility and superb control.

RISING BLOCK/KNIFE HAND STRIKE

The top right picture shows the model on the right blocking a punch from his opponent using a rising block technique. Notice that after his effective block he is in an ideal position to counterattack. This ability to think ahead is a vital part of free sparring.

Try this blocking technique with a friend. Stand in a natural stance. Your friend should make the first move, striking out to punch you while moving his weight forward onto his left leg.

Moving forward onto your right leg block his punch using the rising block technique. Repeat this procedure until you are both fairly proficient. Switch roles occasionally. The bottom right picture shows the counterattack of the model who has successfully blocked his opponent's punch. He retaliates with a knife hand strike (shuto uke) to the side of the face.

The hips are important in this counterattack. They should determine part of the pace and power of the strike. Do not make contact.

FRONT KICK/SIDE KICK

The picture on the opposite page shows a typical free sparring situation. The model on the right counters a front kick (mae-geri) from the model on the left with a masterful side kick (yoko geri kokumi). As with all karate movements, part of the effectiveness of the counterattack lies in split-second timing and the ability to guess the intended actions of your opponent.

This counterattack also calls for tremendous control of mind so that your body is galvanized into action when an opening is presented. The ability to be able to do this takes much practice and is not as easy as it looks.

To find out how true this is, try this whole technique with a friend. Ask him or her to 'attack' you with a front kick. React with a side kick to the chin. You will notice that you will have difficulty with your timing. The only way to master this is through constant repetition.

When you feel that you have learned this counterattack to a reasonable level of competence try switching roles with your friend. Allow him or her to master the difficulty of timing a counterattack. Then try to think of ways to make your initial attack effective so that your friend's counterattack is thrown off balance or deflected.

STEPPING PUNCH/REVERSE PUNCH

The above four pictures show a more complicated piece of free sparring involving four techniques in an attack and counterattack situation. The top left picture depicts the beginning of the attack. The model on the left attacks his opponent with a stepping punch (oi zuki jodan). In the top right picture his opponent completes a brilliant circular sweeping block to deflect the punch, leaving him in a position of tactical superiority.

The bottom left picture shows the position of the opponents just after the circular sweeping block. The model on the right prepares his counterattack.

The bottom right picture depicts just how powerful his counterattack can be. A reverse punch is delivered with great force and good timing. This has proved his block and counter sequence effective. Practise these techniques with a friend, taking care not to land any actual punches.

KIAI

One of the most difficult points to illustrate to a new student is the use of the karate shout (Kiai).

The shout should not come from the throat but should develop from the stomach and explode from the mouth at the instance of attack or defence.

This method of shouting is not peculiar to karate. It is also used by many modern sportsmen such as javelin throwers and weight lifters to enable them to produce more strength from their efforts. The ancient warriors—such as the American Indians and the samurai—shouted as they ran towards their foe, enabling them to gain courage and fight with spontaneity.

The karate student should use kiai with as much fervour as possible and should be aware of its effect.

SIDE STEP/KNIFE HAND STRIKE

The top left picture on the opposite page shows the two models in the free style stance. This stance is normally used in all free sparring contests and is the basis for all attack and defence techniques.

The top right picture depicts the initiation of the attack. The model on the right launches a kick while the model on the left side steps and catches his opponent's leg at the same time. With split-second timing he is ready to counterattack.

The large picture shows the completion of the counter technique. The model on the left uses a knife hand strike to overcome his opponent.

This whole sequence requires great co-ordination and balance to execute effectively.

Try it for yourself to appreciate the difficulties. The start of the counterattack is a crucial part of the movement. You should automatically be in a position where you can strike with the weight of your body behind your hand.

FOOT SWEEP/REVERSE PUNCH

This sequence is more difficult than it looks from the pictures. To perform it effectively calls for good judgement of your opponent's balance. The final carry through should only be executed when you realize you can bring him down using the momentum of his balance.

The large picture above shows the model on the left blocking a punch and moving in for a side sweep. The picture on the left depicts the model on the right being swept upwards and to the side.

The large picture on the opposite page illustrates the completion of the side sweep and the preparation for the counterattack.

A reverse punch to the head finishes the counter sequence and shows the model, on the right of the small picture on the opposite page, in a defeated position.

If you are trying this sequence with a friend you are advised to be as careful as possible, particularly when hitting the floor and delivering the punch.

KARATE AND THE MARTIAL ARTS

Many of the Oriental martial arts are related to karate. Such disciplines as Tai Chi, aikido, judo, wing chun and kenpo have many similarities in style to many of the karate techniques.

This is one of the great assets of learning karate. When you have reached a certain level of competence you can proceed to master another martial art. Judo, for example, is a complete art in its own right and at the same time is a perfect complement to karate. You can sometimes use its techniques to make your style of karate even more effective and colourful to watch.

At the same time, it is often inadvisable to start learning other disciplines while you are still concentrating on karate. It is possible that you may be distracted.

Karate-4

The rewards gained by those who practise the art of karate have been testified to over hundreds of years. Although its benefits have always been extolled, its techniques have largely been kept secret. The ancient karate masters regarded their ways of fighting as a great conferring of power on those who were initiated into its mysteries. They would not submit their learning of the martial arts to documentation in case it fell into the hands of the many gangs of bandits who roamed ancient China.

The traditional and generally accepted theory attributes the introduction of karate into China to Daruma, an Indian monk who ventured across India to China on a spiritual journey. He encountered many difficulties during his travels. But through his tremendous tenacity of mind and body succeeded to pass through bandit-infested country, eventually to arrive at the Shao Lin monastery in northern China.

While staying at the Shao Lin monastery he discovered that many of the monks were very weak, both physically and mentally. He imposed a strict and vigorous training schedule from which the monks gained tremendous strength and stamina of body and great power of mind.

By studying and then adapting many animal fighting positions as well as practising existing combat techniques, the Shao Lin monks soon became the most feared fighters in China.

To ensure the perpetuation of his martial techniques, Daruma evolved a system of teaching using kata, breakdowns of all the movements into set pieces performed by the student alone. It was from these kata that an encyclopedia of karate techniques was passed down through the ages by the ancient masters.

The ancient martial techniques reached one of their most important stages of development on the island of Okinawa when the local feudal lord banned the use of weapons, giving rise to the use of empty hand techniques of fighting. Many local techniques were evolved and blended with the Shao Lin methods. With the continued practice of kata and the toughening of certain parts of the body, the Okinawins became formidable fighters even against opponents carrying weapons.

Kata were of tremendous importance in teaching these techniques. The student always practised kata alone and, by fighting imaginary foes, could train without the hindrance and necessity of other students.

The Okinawins gave their martial art the name of 'Chinese hand' because of the country of its origin. And it was the man to whom karate owes its tremendous growth in modern times who changed the name to 'empty-hand' (kara-te). Master Funakoshi Gichin chose the name from the Buddhist philosophy of 'rendering oneself empty'. To him, karate was not only a martial art but also a means of character development. He wrote, 'As a mirror's polished surface reflects whatever stands before it and a quiet valley carries even small sounds, so must the student of karate render his mind empty of selfishness and wickedness in an effort to react appropriately towards anything he might encounter. This is the meaning of kara (empty) in karate'.

Funakoshi, who died in 1955 at the age of 88, first introduced the modern form of karate to the Japanese public in 1922. His exhibitions of traditional martial arts so impressed his audiences that he was flooded with requests to teach karate in Tokyo. He established his own school and called it the Shotokan. Shoto was his nickname while kan means school. Shotokan is the most widely taught form of karate in use in the West and is the technique presented in this series.

Parts of some of the Shotokan kata are shown in this part of the karate course. Kata are the very foundations of karate and are not only practised by students. Even karate masters continue to perform them.

The applications of some of the kata movements are also shown in the following pages, demonstrating how the techniques can be used in combat. In the performance of kata, a student incorporates all the blocks, forwards and backwards stepping movements, jumps, kicks, punches and striking techniques common to karate.

As you can see from the pictures, the component parts of kata are beautiful to look at and display a unique balance and symmetry of form. By practising them you can radically improve your posture and learn to move with a fluid and controlled mobility. The kata are superior to many forms of exercise and movement in existence today. Many benefits can be gained from learning them.

Kata require much practice and a great deal of dedication to perfect to their highest pitch. But they are the whole basis of karate technique and as such are an important part of a student's training. Although they will demand much of your practice time, they are a joy to learn and perform. Your proficiency at kata will to a great extent determine your proficiency at the application of karate techniques.

There are too many kata to present in a short course. The kata movements presented in this part of the course are intended as an introduction. Practise them as often as you can to appreciate just how beneficial they can be. You will want to learn more.

THE NIJU SHIHO KATA

This sequence from the Niju Shiho kata demonstrates a simultaneous block and strike while turning to face an attacker who approaches from behind.

The picture above shows the kata stance. Try it for yourself. Stand with your legs apart, the forward knee should be bent and the trailing leg should be at a 45 degree angle to your body. The front arm should be held outstretched and pointed upwards. The trailing arm should be held in a similar position behind your back but should point downwards with the palm facing up.

When you have tried the stance relax and return to a normal standing stance.

Then try to jump into the Niju Shiho position shown above. It will take some practice to perfect your balance and symmetry.

The top left picture on the opposite page shows an attacker approaching from behind. The model on the right is aware of his approach and prepares to meet the attack.

The bottom left picture on the opposite page demonstrates the use of the Niju Shiho position in effectively blocking the attack and countering with a strike.

Try this sequence with a friend, being careful not to make any hurtful contact when you swing around. You will find that the technique is not as easy as it looks and will require practice.

Occasionally change roles to appreciate both sides of the movement.

YOGA AND KARATE

Karate requires great suppleness and mobility of the limbs. Many students find that when they are beginning to learn even the basic techniques their muscles and joints become stiff after short periods of practice.

To be able to raise either leg above the horizontal, to squat on the heels or to pivot the pelvis and balance on one leg are all difficulties which the beginner will encounter and must overcome.

Many of the postures of hatha yoga are a perfect form of complementary training to the karate movements. They will provide you with both suppleness and strength so that your karate practice sessions will become easier. And you will master karate more quickly besides learning another discipline.

THE HEAN YONDAN KATA

This part of the Hean Yondan kata can be used as a block and a knife hand strike to an attacker's neck. The model on the left in the picture below shows the kata position. His weight is pressed forwards over his left leg. His right knee is slightly bent to allow great mobility when lunging forwards.

The palm of his attacking hand is turned upwards with the thumb tucked in.

Try this position on your own and then practise the application with a friend. Your friend should 'attack' you with a forward punch which you should try to block.

25

THE NIJYU SHIHO KATA

The top three pictures show three movements from the Nijyu Shiho kata.

The picture on the left depicts a stance which requires a great deal of balance and control.

The centre position demonstrates the progression of the kata. The model has kicked sideways with his right foot while at the same time has clenched his right fist and held it close to his shoulder.

The picture on the right shows the concluding part of the sequence. The model has returned his foot to the ground and used the momentum generated by this action to swing his left arm in a punching motion.

This part of the Nijyu Shiho kata demands a high degree of control. Try it for yourself.

You will find most difficulty in trying to kick sideways. Allow the upper part of your body to keel over with its own weight. Be more concerned with stopping this motion at the correct angle than with actually executing the kick.

The bottom three pictures demonstrate the application of this part of the Nijyu Shiho kata.

The picture on the left shows the first part of the kata being used to block a punch.

After having successfully blocked his opponent's punch, the model on the right counterattacks with a side kick to the stomach—using the second part of the kata. This is shown in the centre picture.

The picture on the right depicts the second part of the counterattack. The model on the right follows his side kick with a punch to the stomach of his opponent.

When you feel that you have mastered the fundamentals of the kata sequence, try applying its techniques in a sparring situation with a friend. Be careful when you are doing this. There are so many movements involved that it is easy to miscalculate a punch or kick and end up with an injury. For this reason take things very slowly and softly at first. Only when you see a marked improvement in your style should you increase your speed.

How often should you practise the karate techniques? What amount of time should you devote to individual training sessions?

The time you give to karate will largely depend on your own preferences and life style. If you join a club many of your sessions will be organized for you and you should have no difficulty in finding a teacher who can arrange your training periods at times which are most suited to you.

If you wish to train at home it is completely up to you as to how much time you give to the karate techniques. Your strength and how easily you become fatigued will determine the length of a session. So will your spirit of dedication influence the pace of learning. When you first start to learn karate you will have to devote a good deal of your time to training.

THE KANKU-DAI KATA (1)

The picture on the right shows a position from the Kanku-dai kata. All of your weight should be placed onto your left leg. Stretch your right leg backwards as far as you can. Turn the toes of your right foot outwards so that the edge of your foot is nearest to the ground. Position your hands as shown by the model. The picture below depicts how this part of the Kanku-dai kata can be applied in a fighting situation. The model on the right attacks with a punch. The model on the left blocks his punch and counters with a simultaneous strike to the groin. He can continue this movement by gripping the inside of the leg and throwing his opponent to the ground. Be careful when trying this.

THE KANKU-DAI KATA (2)

This is a variation of the kata shown on the previous page and demonstrates how an opponent can be thrown off balance and flung to the ground. The picture on the left shows the progression of the movement. The model demonstrates the kata form of the technique used in the picture below. After having 'struck' to the groin he catches his opponent's knee while still blocking the punch. His opponent is now off balance and at his mercy.

The top picture on the opposite page shows the model on the left continuing to grip his opponent's leg, raising it until he has lost his balance and is rendered ineffective as depicted in the bottom picture on the opposite page.

When trying this whole movement with a friend, it is important that you be extremely careful especially when throwing him to the ground. There is a danger that either of you could injure your neck or even break a rib. Once again, go through this sequence slowly, never increasing the speed of execution until you are fairly proficient and feel sure that you land smoothly and with a great deal of care.

When you have finished this part of the Kanku-dai kata, attempt to link it up with the movements shown on the previous page. The movements are not as difficult as in some other karate techniques so that you should learn it fairly quickly.

Practise this and other kata sequences as much as you can. There are many more kata which you will have to learn if you wish to continue to master the techniques of karate and achieve a black belt.

Because kata are a very important aspect of karate it is advisable to learn them from a karate master (sensei). In this way you will not learn the incorrect techniques from the start. If you do learn wrongly you will have difficulties eradicating mistakes from your movements.

This is because each movement you learn should be practised until it becomes second nature.

MOVING ZEN

Many karate students train·for years and still do not master the zen philosophy behind karate. The karate student should strive to be in complete control of both his mind and body so that each works in harmony with the other. A timid or shy person, for example, would learn to shut out these feelings and remain calm and aware. An aggressive person would learn to control his impulsive desire to attack. On the other hand, anger produces a great deal of strength and power. The karate student should develop his mind to such a degree that he can summon anger when he wants to. Yet he should be able to retain an inward calmness so that he can ascertain everything that happens.

Mind development is far harder than learning techniques.

Karate-5

Karate provides you with an excellent means of defence in case of attack. It does not confer any kind of magical invincibility but nevertheless gives you a great amount of superiority.

The philosophy behind karate does not advocate the indiscriminate use of martial skills but stipulates that if there is little choice they should be employed with as much fervour as possible. And it is not paranoid to admit the possibility, however small, that you could be attacked sometime in your life or that you will need to defend others. The ever-increasing amount of violent assaults on ordinary law-abiding citizens reported in newspapers and on television magnifies this possibility of danger.

It is of great importance to stress that it is better to avoid trouble if at all possible. The best form of defence against attack is either to run or try any means of persuasion. If an attacker demands your money, for example, hand it over. Your health is priceless. Any dangerous situation you may find yourself in will dictate your reactions. If it reaches a point where you have to fight, karate will greatly enhance your chances.

When you commence to learn karate, you must be prepared to master the combat techniques of your art.

SITUATION ONE

The pictures on this and the opposite page demonstrate a technique which can be applied if you are attacked in a car—by a hitch-hiker, for example. Although the possibility of this occurring is small, it is best to know what to do.

The picture above shows the attacker making his first move by gripping the driver around the neck while the car is stationary.

The first move of self-defence is depicted in the bottom picture. The driver tightens his neck muscles and pushes his shoulders upward to avoid strangulation.

The top picture on the opposite page shows the driver manoeuvring into a position from which he can counterattack.

The bottom picture on the opposite page shows the vital part of the driver's self-defence. Using his left hand he thrusts two fingers into the eyes of the assailant. If he misses at his first attempt he will try again until the attacker releases his grip. One of the most important reactions in this situation is the driver's initial response. He should grip the steering wheel with his right hand to avoid being dragged into the back seat of the car.

SITUATION TWO

The pictures on these two pages illustrate a situation in which there are two attackers.

The top picture on the left shows the two assailants completing the first part of their attack. The assailant on the right approaches with a knife allowing his partner to grip the intended victim in an arm lock. The centre picture on the left depicts the first move at self-defence. When the assailant wielding the knife comes within striking distance a circular kick is the most effective way to disarm him.

The bottom picture on the left shows how the attacker on the right is finally overcome. A thrust kick to the stomach, applied with great force, renders him incapable of continuing the attack.

The top two pictures on the opposite page depict the downfall of the assailant with the knife and the beginning of the counterattack against his partner.

The centre picture on the opposite page shows the 'victim' turning into the arm lock and immediately reversing the turn with the aid of his hips and shoulders so that the attacker's arm is pulled over his head.

The bottom two pictures on the opposite page depict the concluding stages of the counterattack. By keeping hold of the second attacker's arm the 'victim' throws him off balance and grips him by the back of the neck while at the same time knees him in the face to crush the attack.

The most important part of this self-defence technique is to be aware of the position of the knife at all times. Speed and surprise are essential if the two attackers are to be repelled effectively.

WEAPONS

Against an unarmed attacker, the person who is proficient at karate has a decided advantage. If the attacker wields a knife or any other kind of weapon, however, he must be extremely careful about how he applies his self-defence techniques.

Even a person who uses a knife with little skill can be a source of great danger. By merely waving the knife across the body of the person he is attacking he can inflict a good deal of damage.

Great speed and agility will be called for in overcoming the advantage he has.

Develop these qualities by dedicated training.

33

SITUATION THREE

The technique used in the defence and attack situation shown on these two pages is a very advanced one. It should only be attempted if proficiency at kicking has been attained. If an unskilled person tries to use it he will place himself in a position of extreme vulnerability to serious injury.

The above picture shows a man who suspects that an attacker is waiting around a corner, possibly armed. The top picture depicts the assailant approaching. The intended 'victim' remains as quiet as possible so that he can hear all the movements of his attacker.

The picture on the bottom right shows the 'victim' moving into a suitable posture from which he can kick. He then waits until the assailant appears around the corner.

The picture on the opposite page illustrates how the attacker is repelled. Notice that the attacker is still armed. It is therefore extremely important that the kick is fast and very forceful. It should be strong enough to push the attacker off balance and put him in great pain so that the follow through attack can be made easily. If the kick is forceful it becomes all that much easier to wrench his grip from the knife.

Kung fu-1

The term kung fu does not mean Chinese fighting as is mistakenly thought by many people. It is merely a phrase that implies ability, hard work, task and exceptional or special skills. It is also a generic term for exercise. The normal term of reference for Chinese fighting methods is chung-kuo chu'an which simply means Chinese fist, or hand. There are probably as many styles of Chinese boxing as there are styles of karate, and each individual style incorporates techniques from the others. Most styles, however, include some combat moves common to all the fighting styles to be found on the Chinese mainland.

China, a highly populated country of immense size, has a long and often poorly recorded history dating back to well before the Christian Era. Due to this lack of written information, the origins of Chinese boxing or kung fu, as it is more commonly known in the western world, are very difficult to ascribe with any great authority. It is however, like karate, popularly associated with the Shoa Lin Monastery and the travelling monk Bhodidharuma. (See Karate section).

The development of kung fu is related to the regions from which the various styles originated. In mountainous northern China, for example, where heredity and everyday life combined to produce strong legs among the local inhabitants, styles concentrating on legs and feet were developed with names like wing chum, pa kia, tam tuie, praying mantis and monkey. In the south, among the paddy fields, where the majority of the local inhabitants worked or travelled in or on the water and thus developed strong arms, the upper part of their bodies tended to be the part utilized in fighting techniques. Here names like hung gar, white crane, dragon, mot gar and choy lag just are common.

Despite these many variations, the systems may be divided into two main sections, external and internal. All individual styles either utilize the theory embraced by one section entirely or adapt and intermix parts of both. The external is best described as the hard, aggressive and vigorous side of kung fu, where practitioners appear to be openly hostile. The internal is a soft and pliable style of fighting, where the practitioner appears to be defensive when fighting and yields to his attackers before striking with his own counter move. It must, however, be repeated that many systems of kung fu employ both the external and internal methods.

The practice and display of forms enjoy immense popularity amongst kung fu practitioners. These forms (kata's as they are called in karate) show the many graceful animal-like movements which are incorporated into each style. They display the graceful flowing techniques, agile movements and delicate control necessary to fulfil the demanding standards of the combat situations they simulate. Some forms are hard and fast while others are soft and show great suppleness in their execution.

Kung fu forms, like karate katas, are methods of training that can be practised either individually or in groups. Through them a kung fu practitioner may strengthen his technique, increase his concentration, afford himself suppleness, stamina, and allow himself to give full rein when unleashing blows in the full knowledge that no one need be hurt in the process.

Kung fu is closely related to the Zen philosophy. As was mentioned earlier, the innovation of Chinese boxing stemmed from the monks of the Shoa Lin Temple who worked arduously from dawn till dusk and then spent many long hours in silent meditation. It was not the philosophy of the old Chinese masters to openly display their incredible fighting ability. When, for example, a local warlord, King Idsuan of Chou, heard of a renowned fighter named Po-Kung, he summoned him to his court. When he first saw him he was aghast at the frailness of the man before him. On being asked about his reputed strength Po simply and meekly said, 'I can withstand the wings of an autumn cicada and snap the leg of a spring grasshopper.' The king in reply roared 'I can pull ten grown buffaloes by the tail and can tear the hide of a rhinoceros with my bare hands, and still I am shamed by my weakness. Why is it that you are so renowned?' Po answered, 'I was taught by Tsu-Shang-Chini whose strength and power was without parallel throughout the world, yet even his relatives never knew, because he never used it.'

Recently, due to the amount of television and cinema coverage given to Kung-Fu, interest in it has grown at a remarkable rate. Many of its benefits can be appreciated by the modern individual who is prepared to study and work extremely hard. He will be rewarded by the immense sensation of satisfaction and accomplishment kung fu will afford its devotee. In the following pages are illustrated the many styles and techniques of kung fu that will help you gain a fuller understanding of the art.

THE TIGER TAIL KICK

This picture depicts a tiger tail kick, this is a very strong backward kicking technique where the legs are slammed out hard and fast, like a tiger's tail.

THE DEVELOPMENT OF KUNG FU

The development of Chinese boxing was greatly encouraged by the numerous wars and battles that regularly engulfed the various clans throughout China's long and arduous past. A traditional Chinese boxer can not be compared to a modern western boxer, who is only allowed to use hand punching techniques under close supervision. Conventional Chinese boxing is an art of self defense incorporating various kicking, punching, striking, grappling, wrestling and throwing techniques. The defeat of the opponent is the main aim no matter what length a fighter has to go to overcome his opponent. Techniques such as scratching, biting, eye-gouging can be readily utilized if the more orthodox methods are failing to show results. The kung fu practitioner must also be adept in the use of one or more weapons such as the bow, sword, staff or similar instrument lest he be challenged to dual not only with his hands and feet but also with a weapon.

38

THE HAMMER BLOW

The picture on the left depicts a hammer blow being delivered to the head of one exponent. Note however that the knee and left hand of the defender are placed in such a position that they afford some degree of protection. Remember, one blow will not necessarily render an individual helpless. One should always be ready to follow through.

THE CRANE STANCE

The picture below depicts a classical form stance based on a fight between a tiger and a crane. Note how, in immitation of a crane the exponent stands on one leg and has his hands and arms poised in imitation of wings. It is quite common for kung fu fighting poses to be based on various animal characteristics.

THE SOUTHERN FIGHTING STANCE

The photograph below shows a kung fu fighting stance from the south of China. The legs form a rock like base while the hands and arms are ready to fire punches at an incredible speed, they are also in a position to block any attack.
The Southerners preferred to use their hands and arms while fighting.

Kung fu-2

If you wish to learn kung fu the first step is to find a good and reputable teacher. A teacher who is not only a skilful practitioner but who also possesses the ability to pass his knowledge on. Once such a man is located, then you are on the road to a better and fuller understanding, not only of your physical capabilities but of your own mind.

Initially training will consist of learning the techniques. The constant repetition of these exercises is required before any degree of skill can be attained. Next the application of each technique will be explained. Then working with a partner, each move and counter-move will be practised time and time again. Eventually each movement can be executed without conscious effort. Following this will be form practice, learning each sequence and then spending many long hours in an effort to perfect them. Forms will be continued, until the student can perform them with strength, grace and harmony; until he can begin to comprehend the philosophy of the great masters that lie behind forms.

Finally kung fu practitioners will graduate to free practice. In many kung fu schools, body armour, head gear, gloves, shin pads and shoes are worn, allowing the students to practice their kicking, punching and striking techniques against each other. The reality of a combat situation is thus created, giving the fighters a greater understanding of their techniques and, enabling them to accept some body punishment without undue injury.

Once you have chosen which style and system of kung fu to learn, the rewards

THE FLYING SIDE KICK

This picture depicts a spectacular flying side kick. Such jumping techniques were generally used to leap over obstacles such as downed adversaries or to knock opposing horsemen from their saddles. In many instances flying techniques were used against the horses themselves. A skilled kung fu practitioner would be as knowledgeable about the vulnerable points of a horse as he would be of the vulnerable parts of a man.

THE STRAIGHT PUNCH

The picture to the right shows a strong mid-section straight punch being delivered to the solar plexus region. Such a blow might temporarily deprive a person of the power to breath and should therefore not be attempted.

gained from your training vary directly in proportion to the amount of time and effort you are prepared to invest. Finally you will gain complete control of both your physical and mental being.

In explaining the fighting techniques of kung fu it is necessary to understand the internal and external methods also referred to as yin and yang.

Briefly, the internal systems concentrate on bringing strength from within, yielding from an attack and then seemingly effortlessly overcoming the aggressor. Relaxation and breathing control are two important factors. Circular techniques are also used, involving catching a direct attack and pulling the power of the attack round and past the defender thus meeting the hard with the soft. Another example of this technique is to begin a counter-move after an attack has started, but arriving before the termination of the attack. These are but a few interpretations of the internal method.

The sensation of fighting some one employing the internal method is similar to the sensation of falling into a pool. The water offers no resistance to entry but once immersed one is completely controlled by its movements, be it rough or calm. In the same way, though little resistance is offered against the aggressor he soon falls into the power of the defender.

The external may be described as the strong, direct, aggressive form of kung fu, taking its strength from without and meeting force with force to overcome an aggressor. Both the internal and external methods are very complex and closely overlap each other, thus to draw a clear dividing line between one and the other is almost impossible. It is sufficient to say that for anyone who wishes to learn kung fu it will be necessary to train for many years before a degree of understanding of these two highly complex systems is gained.

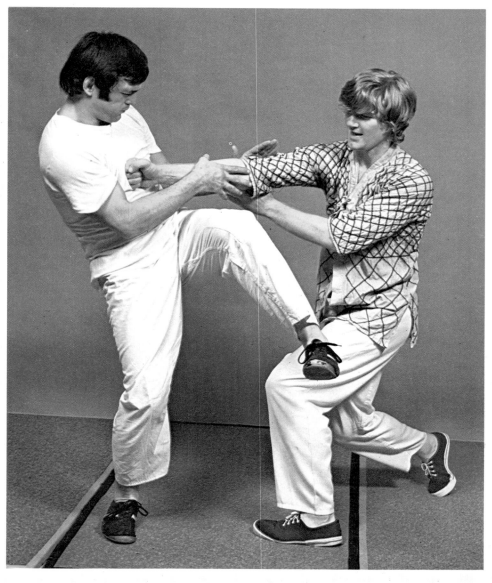

THE SCISSORS TAKE DOWN

The above picture shows the execution of a flying scissors take down. The exponent on the left has leapt forward opening his legs in a scissors motion. Upon contact his opponent would become ensnared, brought to the ground and at once rendered powerless.

THE FOLLOW UP

The bottom right picture depicts the follow up to the scissors take down. Notice the left hand held firmly and the knife hand attack directed straight to the throat. A skilled kung fu practitioner is always ready to follow up one swift move with another.

THE NORTHERN STANCE

The picture on the top right shows a kung fu fighting stance from the mountainous north of China. Each exponent is crouched low yet is capable of springing forward at tremendous speed. The style is imitative of a tiger, an animal once common in the north.

DEFENSE
The picture to the left depicts two exponents using their front legs and arms to protect and shield otherwise vulnerable areas. Although it is theoretically possible to execute a foot sweep to the supporting leg, it must be remembered that each exponent will move with great speed.

THE COUNTER
The picture below gives an excellent view of a kick being countered by the left arm of the man on the right also the simultaneous strike with the other hand. It can be seen however that the other man has avoided it and palm blocked the attack.

JUMPING TECHNIQUE
The picture to the right depicts another jumping technique, this one is a flying hammer blow to the head. This type of technique would be used against an armed attacker as he thrust past.

Judo 1

Judo is an exciting, invigorating and very enjoyable modern day sport. It is derived from ju-jitsu, the ancient art of unarmed combat.

Traditionally it was brought to Japan by the Chinese monk, Chin Gendin, yet little is known for certain. Whatever its precise origins, however, ju-jitsu rapidly grew in popularity and spread throughout Japan. The numerous civil wars and clan feuds that beset Japan until modern times, further extended its importance. Knowledge of one of the many schools of ju-jitsu was thus a vital facet of any samurai's (knight's) training in the age of Japanese chivalry. An ordinance of 1871 forbidding the samurai to carry swords further encouraged the learning of ju-jitsu.

The sport of judo was formulated by Dr Jiguro Kano at the end of the nineteenth century and became popular in the West. Due to his efforts, it was the first oriental martial art to gain world wide appeal.

A new student of judo will at once be caught in the tremendous atmosphere of this sport from the first day he enters the dojo (training hall). He will find the rewards and satisfaction of his ever-increasing proficiency a life-long boon. According to Doctor Kano, "judo is the means of understanding the way to make the most effective use of both physical and spiritual power and strength. By devoted practice and rigid discipline in an effort to attain perfection in attacking and defending, it refines the body and soul and helps instil the spiritual essence of judo into every part of one's very being. In this way it is possible to perfect oneself and contribute something worthwhile to the world."

The techniques of judo are numerous and the use of a particular move depends entirely on the situation presented. The very essence of judo is the skilful application of the power of resistance combined with the utilization of the disorientating effect of yielding, using skilful technique to overcome brute strength.

The art of judo lies in the ability of the individual to interpret the body movements of his opponent. For example, if a man possessed the strength of three and his opponent the strength of two, the stronger man would invariably win. However, if the weaker man combined his strength with his opponent's by pushing when the stronger pulls, he could double his strength and easily knock the stronger man to the ground.

This is one of the fundamentals of good judo technique and it is the gaining of this skill in practice, combined with the graceful execution of each movement when competing with an opponent, which gives the individual such fulfilment and release from tension.

THE ALL JAPAN CHAMPIONSHIPS
The famous All Japan championships were inaugurated in 1948. They are championships with no weight category, and as a result – although men of all sizes and weights are theoretically equal – a big man has invariably won the title, the victor's average weight since 1948 being 15 stone. The championships are the highlight of the Japanese judo calendar, and the participants qualify through a series of regional eliminations. The early rounds provide much of the most exciting judo, and once the pressure increases in the final stages the fighters become less adventurous.

NATURAL PREPARATION
The picture to the left shows two jukoka in the correct natural standing position. In this posture both grasp the other's left sleeve and right collar in an effort to secure the firm hold so necessary for a strong throw and good defense. Strong hands and well developed arms assist greatly in natural preparation for a throw or knock down.

THE TAI-TOSHI
The picture to the right shows the position for tai-toshi (body drop). In this throw the exponent on the right has extended his right foot across the front of his opponent. It is important to retain a firm hold in order to execute the throw.

THE FOLLOW THROUGH
The picture to the left depicts the follow through to the tai-toshi shown on the previous page. The exponent on the right follows his fist move by slamming his hip into his opponent and pulling forward towards the ground.

THE TERMINATION
This final picture shows the termination of the throw, notice the outstretched hand of the exponent being thrown. By slapping his arm and hand to the ground at the moment of impact he can break the main force of the fall. It is important that a judoka never ceases to practise break falls such as this.

DR JIGORO KANO
Few men have worked so hard to popularize a new sport as Dr Jogoro Kano, the founder of judo. Kano graduated from the Imperial University in Tokyo in 1881, and feeling a need for more physical exercise attended several ju-jitsu schools. After an examination of the techniques involved, he welded the best principles of each into a system he called 'judo' – literally 'easy way', but interpreted by Kano as 'maximum efficiency'. In 1882, he founded the first Kodokan or judo school, at Shitaya.

Dr Kano was able to watch the sport rapidly expanding, and he published numerous books on the subject. But he envisaged judo more as a training for life and not solely as a sport in isolation. He himself spoke perfect English – a rare accomplishment for a Japanese in those days – and was the headmaster of two distinguished Japanese high schools.
Kano was also responsible for founding the Japanese Olympic Committee, and he died at sea in 1938 returning from the Cairo International Olympic Conference.

Judo 2

The five main judo techniques

1 Ukemi break falls It is essential at the outset of judo training to learn how to fall correctly. The possibility of being thrown to the ground from almost any angle must be taken into consideration when practising break falls. It is necessary to start learning falls slowly and from a low level, gradually building up speed and height, changing the angle of fall until the judoka (judo-student) gains skill and confidence in almost every falling situation he finds himself in. Only when he has complete confidence in his ability to fall without fear of injury will a judoka be able to act positively when competing with an opponent.

2 Throwing techniques Throwing techniques are the very basis of judo and it is the appeal of being able to compete both mentally and physically with an opponent without fear of serious injury that has given judo its world-wide popularity.

There are numerous throwing movements, each one based on respective parts of the thrower's body, hand techniques such as tai-toshi (body drop), sedi-nage (back-carry throw) where the main emphasis is on a very strong hand grip and use of the arms to throw an opponent. The shoulders also play a vital role in the preparation and execution of hand techniques.

Hip techniques such as harai-goshi (hip sweep), and hane-goshi (hip spring) are among the strongest judo throws, where the judoka slams his hip into his opponent and then pivots him over the top or side. Leg techniques are also among the strong take-down moves and include techniques such as osoto-gare (big outside drop), deashi-barai (forward foot sweep) and oguruma (big whirl) where either the leg or foot is used to sweep the opponent to the floor.

Other important throws are rear and side fall throws, such as tomoe-nage (round throw) and tani-otoshi (valley drop), sometimes known as sacrifice throws, where one exponent throws himself to the ground pulling his partner with him and then flips him over the top.

3 Arm locks and strangle holds Arm locks can be applied whenever and wherever the opportunity arises. Both judoka may still be standing and whilst grappling for a firm hold to aid the execution of a strong throw, one may present an opening for an arm lock to be applied. As it implies, the arm lock is the manipulation of the joint against its natural opening function and when applied is extremely painful.

Strangles are normally applied when both exponents are on the ground although a very skilful judoka may attempt one whilst standing. The strangulation tech-nique is applied by gripping the upper collar of the jacket and with use of the forearm, twisting it tightly around the neck of the opponent thus preventing the blood flow to the brain, resulting in a temporary blackout. This move should never be attempted unless under expert supervision.

4 Ground work After a successful throw has been completed a judo contest is normally concluded, but when one judoka has only managed to knock the other down with an incomplete technique, he must immediately try and pin down his opponent for a stipulated period of time to win the contest.

There are many ways of pinning and holding down an opponent and, of course, many counter moves to these.

5 Atemi-waza Atemi-waza must be considered to be a part of the judoka's repertoire although it is no longer taught to the modern practitioners of judo. This was the art of striking the weak points of an adversary with the hands, feet and head while in actual combat using techniques such as finger stabbing to the eyes and strikes to the groin. Atemi-waza however plays no part whatsoever in contest judo.

If one wishes to achieve both satisfaction and enjoyment from a sport one can not do better than to attain a degree of proficiency in judo. It is however a sport that entails a high degree of risk to its participants if they fail to treat it with respect. Never enact any of the moves shown unless mats are provided and you are under expert supervision.

COUNTER TAI TOSHI

The picture on the left shows the exponent on the left stepping across the front of his opponent in an attempted tai-toshi. All judo throws are capable of being countered before take down, whether or not they are depends largely on the sense of balance of the person concerned, and his state of readiness for the intended counter move. Sometimes a stronger man, by sheer brute strength can stop a throw being made but in certain circumstances the use of all his strength will not hinder but help the throw.

The picture above shows tai-toshi being countered by teguruma. The exponent on the right bends his knees and grips the belt of his opponent in preparation for the counter.

GLOSSARY OF TERMS

Ashiwaza Technique of foot throws.
Chui Warning for an infringement.
Dan Degree.
Dojo Judo practice hall.
Gyaku Reverse – applied to locks, holds, etc.
Ippon One point.
Jigotai Defensive posture.
Judogi Judo costume, loose fitting trousers and jacket without buttons. The jacket is fastened with a belt to assist in identification.
Judoka Person who practises judo.
Kaeshiwaza Counter-attack techniques.
Kata A series of pre-arranged movements. Now performed as a training method and for demonstrations.
Katsu A method of resuscitation.
Koshiwaza Techniques of hip throws.
Kyu Pupil degree.
Newaza Groundwork.
Osaekomiwaza Holding techniques.
Randori Free practice.
Sensei Teacher.
Shiai Contest.
Shihan Master.
Sutemiwaza Sacrifice throws.
Shimewaza Strangulation techniques.
Tachizawa Throwing techniques.
Ukemi Breakfalls.
Waza Technique.

GRADING

The judo grading system enables an individual's skill and experience to be ascertained. Grades are divided into Dan (degree) and Kyu (pupil) sections. A beginner wears a white belt, and after examinations goes through the following states:

    5th Kyu Yellow belt.
    4th Kyu Orange belt.
    (Japan: White belt).
    3rd Kyu Green belt.
    2nd Kyu Blue belt.
    1st Kyu Brown belt.
    (Japan: Brown belt).
    1st Dan Black belt.
    2nd Dan Black belt.
    3rd Dan Black belt.
    4th Dan Black belt.
    5th Dan Black belt.
    6th Dan Red and White belt.
    7th Dan Red and White belt.
    8th Dan Red and White belt.
    9th Dan Red belt.
    10th Dan Red belt.
    11th Dan Red belt.
    12th Dan White belt.

Grades are given according to fighting ability – a contestant has an increasing number of fights as he gains experience – and also on technical knowledge. Above 5th Dan, grades are given for the judoka's contribution to the sport and not on fighting ability. Thus the top international fighters are usually 4th or 5th Dans. Theoretically, it is possible for a person to reach the 12th Dan and receive the White Belt – having done the complete circle in judo – but this honour has never been bestowed. The highest grade ever awarded by the Technical Panel of the Kodokan, the centre of the sport, is the 10th Dan. With the spread of judo, gradings have become less significant, but they are still useful for estimating the level a person has reached in the sport. Downgradings are given only in the event of misconduct. In the late 1960s, the British Judo Association introduced a points system to bring them into line with the rest of Europe and Japan. This enabled a judoka to accumulate points from gradings in major contests for promotion to the next grade. But the kyu gradings are still given at regular three-monthly contests.

THE COUNTER

The picture directly above shows how by straightening his knees and lifting the leg and belt of his opponent the man on the right is capable of countering an attempted throw.

To prevent serious injury all judo training halls (dojos) are covered with either Japanese tetemi (straw fabricated mats) or more modern rubber compound mats. These enable a judoka to fall heavily to the floor and allow the punishment of the throw to be bodily absorbed.

GROUNDWORK

The final picture of the sequence shows the application of ground-work. This is where one opponent tries to pin the other for a period of time in order to gain an advantage.

HOW TO PLAY

The object of a judo competition is to throw one's opponent cleanly, hold him immobile on his back for 30 seconds, forcing him to submit through the pressure of an armlock or stranglehold, or – more usual in top-class competitions – to gain a decision given by two judges and a referee. Only one point – an ippon – is needed to decide a contest, because the theory is that in early times a single clean throw, a stranglehold, or a hold-down could disable a person. The two judges sit at diagonally opposite corners of the mat, and the referee

conducts the contest from the mat itself.

The fighters approach one another, and after a ceremonial bow they take hold of each other by the jacket. They are permitted to grab at the legs or hold the belt to assist with throws. Newaza (groundwork) is resorted to when the competitors fight on the ground. Some competitors specialize in this aspect of the sport and lure their opponents on to the ground and use their strength there.

Most international contests are won on a decision in which a number of knock-downs are counted by the judges. But a waza-ari (almost a point) can be scored which overrules a knock-down. In the event of an equal number of knock-downs and no score on the ground, the contestant who has done most attacking gets the decision. A chui (warning) for an infringement can also decide a close contest when a waza-ari or an ippon have not been awarded.

When practising, judo experts attempt to be more free than in contests. Randori forms the basis of training, but techniques are improved with frequent practice of movements or parts of movements. Weight training and running are part of the training of more ambitious competitors.

Because judo throws are violent, a system of breakfalls has been evolved which allows the expert to soften his own fall. He relaxes and hits the mat with an outstretched arm to prevent any serious damage. Despite its violent nature, judo is a very formal sport. Competitors bow to each other before and after each match, even in training. The instructor is always respected, and people in the higher grades are always honoured. Black belts assist kyu (pupil) grades in their training, as they were once beginners themselves.

Aikido

The literal translation of aikido is; ai (harmony), ki (spirit), do (way), the way of martial spiritual harmony.

This system of defense was originated by the late Master Morihei Uyeshiba, who was born in 1883 at Wakayamama Prefecture in Japan. Master Uyeshiba devoted many long, hard years to the practice and study of several martial arts, before the development of aikido was realized. This new art was not only a form of physical defense and exercise, but also a deeply spiritual activity.

The bodily interpretation of the techniques and disciplines of aikido are but the basis of a truer and more realistic approach to the spiritual harmony of togetherness, helpfulness and understanding, to which all true aikido practitioners strive.

The main schools of aikido philosophy maintain that the secret of this art is the oneness of mind, spirit and body and that the supreme state is to be at one with Nature and the Spirit of the Universe.

While bearing in mind the deeply spiritual aspect of aikido, it must be realized that it is also a profoundly exciting and extremely effective means of self-defense. An aikido practitioner utilizes the power and force offered against him by an aggressor and redirects it to his own account. For example, when an attacker rushes him, he steps aside, catching the

TANTO RANDORI
The picture to the left depicts two aikidoists engaging in tanto randori (free fighting). Here a hip throw is being successfully applied.
The picture below shows an example of tanto tori (knife taking), where one exponent has grasped the wrist of the other in preparation for a following throw.

aggressor's arm and at the same time swinging him in a circle, before flipping him to the ground. An arm or wrist lock is then immediately applied.

The techniques of aikido are many and varied, each individual movement can be easily and swiftly followed by another. Essentially the techniques and movements can be summarized as follows. Firstly the basic knowledge, such as kmae (posture), ma-ai (distance), irimi (entering), ukemi (breakfalls) and chikari no dashikata (extension of power). These are followed by solo exercises (tandoku dosa), which include movements such as breathing and wrist strengthening. After the tandoku dosa come the paired exercises, in which two individuals work with one another, turning and twisting their arms and bodies, in an effort to understand the continuous flow of power necessary for correct aikido technique.

The sequence continues with the wide range of throwing moves (nage waza), such as kaiten-nage (rotary throw) and shiho-nage (four side throw).

Finally the last of the empty hand sections would include, katame waza (hold down techniques) incorporating ude-osae (arm pin) and kote-hineri (wrist twist).

Self-defense for an unarmed man against an assailant armed with a sword, knife or staff is another very important aspect of aikido technique. This type of training is called tanto-tori (knife taking), jo-tori (stick taking) and token-tori (sword taking).

Aikido is the perfect balance between physical and mental control, balance and perfectly timed relaxed movement.

Anyone wishing to acquire a knowledge of self-defense and yet receive an insight into himself and others would be well advised to study the beautiful art of aikido.

In aikido there are numerous ways of defending against an armed attacker, however, it must be realized that only after many years of practice can this type of technique be attempted in free practice. Absolute mind control and a masterly attitude when facing an armed opponent coupled with a steady awareness help even the balance between the armed and unarmed aikidoist. It is very important that untrained people do not attempt these weapon defenses and should seek out a reputable club with qualified instructors who can teach these techniques.

The photograph below illustrates ude-nobashi (arm lock). One exponent has attacked with a knife after skilfully being evaded by the defender and has been pinned with an arm lock.

The shot to the left shows the preparation and posture used before applying nage-waza (throwing technique).

The final picture shows a stepping to the side evasion where the exponent on the left has stepped back and to the side while applying a strong wrist hold.

TOMIKI AIKIDO

The dummy knife contest is a special aspect of Tomiki aikido that has caused controversy among the purists. But Tomiki followers regard the knife merely as an extension of the arm or hand. The same techniques are used whether the assailant is armed or not, and they are just as effective in either case. Furthermore, they say, there is no danger of this kind of aikido being abused or misapplied for aggressive ends because each technique is strictly defensive and based on the assumption that any attacker must make the first move.

The Tomiki system of aikido also differs from Uyeshiba's in that it includes a competitive element. At present, competitions are held annually only between universities in Japan. The Tomiki system is still in an experimental stage, from the competitive aspect, because individuals vary in their aggressiveness. Over-exuberant contestants must be controlled because aikido, unlike other martial arts, concentrates principally on the wrists, elbows, and other joints, and a keen, unskilled novice might inflict serious injury.

In addition to the Uyeshiba and Tomiki systems, there are several other less well-known schools.

Oriental weaponry 1

Armed combat has its origins in the earliest development of man's instinct for survival. The search for food and the necessity to defend his territory against wild animals and other enemies, precipitated the development of a variety of missiles and projectiles, from stones to complex catapults and throwing sticks.

Although the development of man's exploitation of his resources varied enormously throughout the world, there seems to be little variation in the kinds of weaponry which were made and used, in different cultural contexts.

There are several possible explanations for this. Firstly it may be that the materials available and the physical environments were similar. Secondly, it is possible that the process of trial and error, which is an integral part of any discovery, produces similar results in dissimilar contexts. Thirdly, cultural contact, through invasion or commerce, may have offered the opportunity for some peoples to incorporate some features of the weapons of others, or copy them entirely. It is likely however that it is a combination of all three factors which has resulted in these similarities.

Weapons can be divided into two main categories. The first, indirect weapons, contains those which either fire a projectile to destroy their prey, or are the instrument of destruction themselves. These include stones, catapults, spears, bows and arrows, throwing sticks, light and heavy artillery, and finally rockets and bombs. The effectiveness of these weapons depends largely upon how accurately and how far the missile can travel without losing its impact.

The second category contains those weapons which are normally wielded by an individual in close combat. They could also be thrown but this would greatly reduce their effectiveness. This second group is known as direct and includes clubs, knives, swords, sticks, flails and bayonets. In the course of the history of weaponry, the weapons in these categories have been both individually employed and used in conjunction, with equal effect. The relative advantages in using direct or indirect types, depend entirely on the demands of the conflict situation.

These categories can be further subdivided into two sections, that is instruments designed and manufactured specifically for fighting and killing an adversary and, tools and hunting implements adapted for use in conflict.

It is obvious, however, that the overall effectiveness of any weapon depends on the proficiency of the user. Modern weapons, despite electronic guidance systems and computer control, still require highly trained personnel to operate them at their optimum level. However our immediate concern is with the training required to manipulate hand held weapons effectively.

Throughout history, in every culture, warriors have appreciated the importance of practice in the successful handling of weaponry, as well as to the development and perfection of new combat techniques. Through trial and error, they incorporated the most successful moves and strikes into their combat repertoire eventually adopting them permanently. Attacks, blocks and counters were studied and experimented with before being tried in real combat, since in a life and death situation a wrong move or strike, or even a poorly practised combination, could result in serious injury or death. Thus much in the development of hand held weaponry, can be traced to military practice.

However many effective weapons and techniques were the result of the adaptation of the farming implements and household tools used by the peasants, both to till their soil and to defend their homes and property. Their effectiveness was constantly proven in combat situations, and alternative defensive practices became incorporated into the use of weaponry as a result.

Many of these skills and weapons, created out of necessity, have become obsolete in modern times. It is only now that there is a general revival of interest in mastering combat techniques. Some of the weapons, such as the rifle, bow and arrow and pistol, have been adopted for use in modern sporting competitions and have thus continued to develop and improve, but many others have fallen into disuse and the skills forgotten.

This picture depicts an overhead trapping block. The exponent on the left has struck downwards to smash his adversary's head, while the other has caught the staff in the air with the prongs facing upwards. This would be followed by an open bladed strike to the head.
The correct way to use any weapon is to realize first that it is an extension of the body, only in this way will the effectiveness of any individual technique become completely apparent. For example the bo gives the holder additional reach and affords him the ability to strike at an opponent while still out of arms reach.

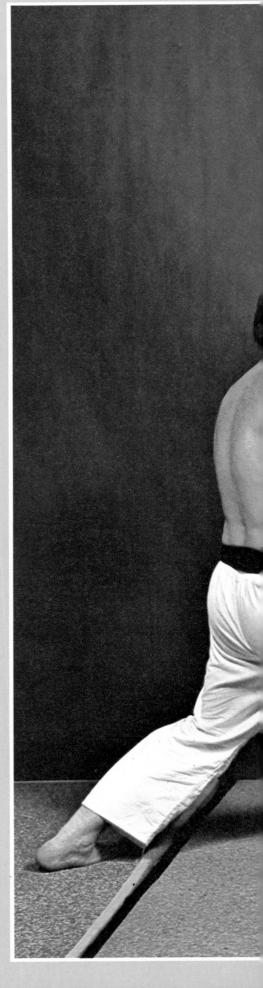

The picture in the top left hand corner shows a classical nun-chaku fighting posture. From this position almost any attack can be anticipated and dealt with.

In the above left picture the assailant on the left has attempted a chudan (centre) slashing cut coming from left to right. His opponent has leapt back to avoid this cut and is trying to smash down his nun-chaku on his attacker's head or wrists.

The picture to the left depicts a jodan block against the staff. Notice how the main shock has been absorbed by the flexible connection between the two nun-chaku sticks.

The above picture follows on from the one to the left. The defender has first blocked a head strike and has trapped the staff by twisting the flexible connection of the nun-chaku around it. He has then, while securing the staff firmly in the nun-chaku, delivered a thrust kick to the head of his assailant (jodan yoko geri ko-komi).

Oriental weaponry 2

Bo-jitsu

The staff or stick has been used as a weapon from man's earliest times. At first it was probably just a branch, hastily trimmed, for use in a defensive situation. Later man became more selective about the type and weight of wood chosen, shaping and hardening his branch to create a specific kind of weapon. The staff has developed as a fighting weapon all over the world.

In appearance the staff does not much resemble a deadly weapon, but in the hands of an expert it can be employed with devastating effects. The many grappling, striking, poking, parrying and defensive techniques associated with the use of the staff, enable a skilled practitioner to defend himself against and defeat an unarmed assailant, with comparative ease.

The choice of wood and the length and weight of the weapon, naturally depend upon the conflict situation. Obviously for optimum efficiency in a situation where the opponent is out of striking distance, a longer lighter staff would be employed. In close combat, the length of staff would decrease proportionately.

Other weapons which are associated with the simple staff are those weapons to which a blade or cudgel has been attached at the end of the pole. The combat techniques employed in the use of these weapons are very similar to that of the staff, although the efficiency of the bladed weapons is increased by their use for cutting and stabbing.

Nunchaku-jitsu

The nunchaku originated in Southeast Asia, where its primary function was as a flail in the cultivation, grinding and polishing of rice. The agricultural workers of this area could not afford, or in many cases were forbidden to carry, more conventional weapons. Thus the adaptation of their many and varied agricultural implements for use as lethal weapons, was a logical and necessary development. The nunchaku is constructed by simply joining two pieces of hard wood of equal length and weight, with cord, horse hair or chains.

The weapon is then used like an extremely flexible whip. It is whirled around at great speed, employing a combination of techniques. It can be used by incorporating clubbing, poking and ensnaring techniques with the traditional flailing moves. In addition its flexible connection can be used as a vice.

The nunchaku has recently been the subject of a great deal of publicity, and with its growing popularity it has also been subject to substantial abuse. It must be stressed that while the nunchaku is a simple weapon, it is like all weapons, extremely dangerous in untrained and unskilled hands. It is potentially lethal not only to an adversary, but also to the inept user.

Jitte or Sai

The jitte or sai is a short, pointed weapon, fashioned from metal. The length and weight are variable but it is normally between fifteen and eighteen inches long and from one to three pounds. The shaft may be pointed or blunt and it generally has two prongs at the point of attachment to the hilt. In practice this is an extremely effective weapon. It is generally used in defence against the sword or staff, as well as in combat with an unarmed assailant. The techniques by which the jitte is used are also varied. It can be wielded like a club or with a punching and stabbing motion. In addition the pronged hilt could be used as a hook to ensnare the opponent's weapon and then counter him.

In the top left hand picture a combined block and counter using sais is depicted. The exponent on the left has attacked with a shomen uchi (head cut) administered by a katan a (samourai sword), while the other is employing a jodan uke (head block). The sai had been flipped from an inverted position to the extended position shown, this gives greater momentum and induces more power in the blow.

The bottom left hand picture shows a block against a katana using the fork pronged hilt to trap the blade after a strike or thrust. This block is applied at the same time as a punching action thus utilizing the end of the handle which is brought to bear against the assailant's head.

The picture above shows both exponents leaping into the air and kicking at the same time. They are using their staffs in a manner similar to that used by a modern pole-vaulter.

This type of technique was principally used to knock horsemen to the ground although it could also be used to gain distance.

The picture above shows the exponent on the left executing a thrusting technique to the head using the end of the staff as the striking area.

The exponent on the right sweeps it to the side using the outside edge of his staff and then stamps the edge of his foot into the knee of his opponent.

The picture to the left depicts an ai-uchi strike, simultaneous blows. At the same time both opponents have struck at each other, one with a head attack and the other with a groin attack. The severity of the blows struck by either exponents would be sufficient to easily down a man.

The above picture depicts a classical overhead block using the centre of the staff. This block is very effective against all attacks coming directly down on to the head or shoulders. Another technique shown by the exponent on the right is the straight head strike while jumping in the air. This is executed either to jump over attacks aimed at the lower limbs, or again to gain distance, and perhaps induce an element of surprise into the attack.

The picture to the right depicts a leg hook and groin strike being applied by the exponent on the right. By pushing at the end of the staff it would be possible to bring the man on the left to the ground. This would be immediately followed by another blow to finish the movement.

The Art of Kendo—1

A modern, disciplined sport, kendo incorporates the superb control of the ancient samurai warrior who moved with remarkable speed and swerve as he cut, parried, evaded and attacked with his sword. An art soaked in tradition, kendo is a perfect balance between physical fitness and delicately-timed movement. A concise and confident mental approach is also involved.

All the qualities of the samurai warrior are called upon in kendo. A disciplined, alert and agile mind directs a well-trained, co-ordinated body in whip-like attacks and parries executed in an instant. The whole body moves the sword in lightning movements, responding to an opponent with split-second timing. The kendo adept reacts with such speed that many of his movements are barely perceptible. This takes some training. But it can be achieved by anybody—even you—with a certain amount of dedication.

The kendo student does not find practice laborious. In fact it is extremely enjoyable. The sheer sense of physical release experienced as you fight an opponent with the minimum of restraint is exhilarating. Kendo students can strike each other many vigorous blows without the fear of injury. This is due to the simple but very effective training armour which is worn and the use of the bamboo sword, called the shinai.

And you can take part in a kendo fight without months of training. Unlike karate and other martial arts, kendo requires a minimum of initial practice before active participation with opponents. The more you practise, of course, the more adept you will become and the more satisfaction you will gain from fighting. But at the outset you do not have to spend months of hard training before being allowed to take part in combat with other people.

Kendo, the way of the sword, originated hundreds of years ago in the ancient feudal system of Japan. It has developed from a lethal fighting art used by the samurai to an exciting and invigorating sport. Kendo as practised today was developed about 200 years ago with the introduction of the bamboo sword (shinai) which was then followed by the use of heavy cloth and bamboo armour. The shinai was first incorporated into the practice sessions of the samurai to prevent injury which could occur when using a real sword.

During the sixteenth century, when Japan was fraught with successive nation-wide civil wars, the techniques of sword fighting were studied as a matter of life and death. The samurai brandished their swords as though extended parts of their arms, learning the many cutting, slicing and thrusting movements of swordsmanship.

With the advent of modern weaponry, the futility of the sword as an effective weapon was recognized. In its place a real and necessary reason for kendo training was substituted. The sword is no longer considered as a means to life or death but as an instrument which will allow the student to strive for the ultimate objective in kendo—physical and mental control. This is achieved with the great enjoyment of fighting.

Kendo training offers a superb system of attaining physical and mental discipline, rewarding the student with self-control, confidence, good manners, fitness and the will to face everyday problems and stress without fear. This, combined with the tremendous sense of satisfaction as your ability increases, is certainly a considerable reason to begin kendo

The simple and enjoyable art of kendo sword fighting offers you confidence and an enjoyable physical skill.

training. Kendo also offers friendship and alliance with the many thousands of other kendo players throughout the world.

This is the first in a series designed to give you some knowledge of what kendo involves. The pictures are modelled by two former members of the British kendo team who have achieved many successes in world competition. The illustrations are exciting and easy to follow.

If you wish to become involved in kendo after reading the series it is advisable to join a club. In the meantime you could practise some of the movements with a broom handle. But do not try any fast swordsmanship. You could do yourself some injury. Rather practise the more 'static' movements such as the basic cuts and parries. Even then be careful and carry out the movements slowly.

The kendo series will show you the basics of the art and the kata movements, stylized postures used in training. Also the history of kendo and the samurai sword will be discussed. You will gain much enjoyment and information about an ancient system of fighting which is now one of the most exhilarating of modern sports.

The picture on the right shows the kendo student's equipment. The armour consists of a mask (men) for protection of the face, head and shoulders, a breastplate (do) which covers the rib cage, breastbone and stomach and can be made of leather-covered bamboo or plastic. An apron (tare) which is made up of five flaps is worn around the hips to protect the thighs and groin. A pair of padded gloves is also worn to cover the hands and wrists. This armour protects the fencer from the shinai, a sword which is constructed from four pieces of bamboo held together in a tubular shape by a small leather cap (saki-gawa) at the top and a leather sheath (tsuka-gawa) at the handle end. These are joined by a string (tsuru) running the length of the shinai and representing the back of the blade. A leather binding about two thirds of the sword's distance from the handle prevents the bamboo from bending outwards. Finally, separating the blade and the handle, a handguard (tsuba) completes the simplicity of the shinai. The shinai is the sword nearest the armour. The towel bearing an insignia shown on the wall is called a tenugui and is worn under the mask to absorb sweat.

The armour is worn over clothing which consists of a heavy cotton short-sleeved jacket (kendogi) and a pair of very wide trousers (ha-kama) resembling a divided skirt.

Kendo involves a great deal of etiquette. This is done out of respect for one's opponent and to ensure that no undue injuries will result while the two fighters are preparing for combat. Although it is not likely that injury will occur nowadays because of the shinai, the samurai swords were so sharp that injury could result just from a touch. After arranging their armour the two fighters on the left compose themselves for combat. Then they bow as shown below.

Kendo etiquette is still observed today in the modern dojo or fighting hall. Kendo aims to instil respect and good manners besides teaching a highly-skilled sport.

After the preliminary bow, the fighters put on their armour. The order of dressing is as follows. The jacket (kendogi) is worn first. This is followed by the trousers (hakama). The waist flaps (tare) are then tied round the hips followed by the breastplate (do). Before placing the mask (men) over the face, the towel (tenugui) is wrapped round the top of the head, covering the hair. Finally the gloves (kote) are worn and the fighter is ready for combat.

The picture on the right shows one model wrapping the towel around his head. His opponent is tying the mask at the back of his neck.

The picture below depicts the two fighters, shinai at their sides, ready for the fight. Even at this stage of preparation etiquette is observed and the opponents show care in how they handle and manipulate the shinai.

Before fencing commences the two opponents face each other, bow and then walk towards each other until they are a few feet apart. Both then squat and draw swords, crossing them as shown in the above picture. Neither fencer can strike until both have risen to the formal fighting stance of chudan no kamae. Again the etiquette of kendo is observed as a sign of mutual respect between the two opponents.

The chudan no kamae or fighting stance is depicted by the models in the picture on the left. Combat must never begin until both fighters have reached this position.

The picture immediately above shows the chudan no kamae from the front. Notice the right foot is always forward. The sword is held by both hands, the right hand held near the guard on the handle and turned slightly upwards. The sword should point at the opponent's throat. This will prevent him from charging in when fighting begins.

The picture immediately below depicts a cut to the head. This is called a shomen. There are various scoring positions on different parts of the body from which superiority is judged in kendo competitions. These include most areas except the thighs, arms and back.

The picture above shows the two fencers observing another part of kendo etiquette. During combat, should any piece of armour come undone, fighting must stop to put the armour right. This ensures that nobody will be hurt through over-enthusiasm. While training, a student will find that his teacher will be strict about this.

The large picture immediately above illustrates a typical free training situation. The model on the right has attacked with a single-handed cut which the fencer on the left tries to evade. The samurai's training included variations of one-handed techniques either to trick an opponent or should one arm be injured during combat. Many such techniques are taught to the student learning the basics of fencing.

The Art of Kendo—2

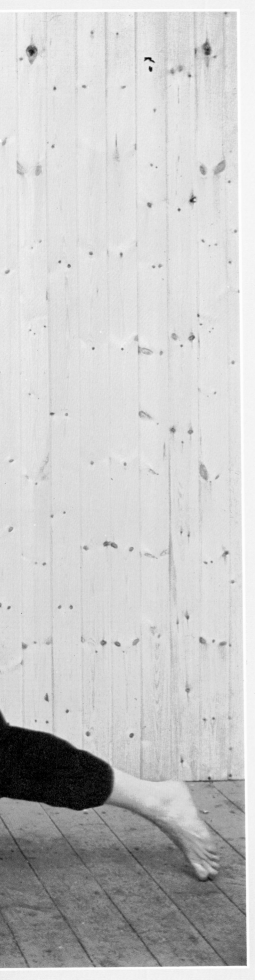

Kendo is an exhilarating and extremely enjoyable sport. Based on the sword fighting techniques of the ancient samurai, it requires patience, discipline, determination and a willingness to learn and benefit from the experience of physical and mental training. In return it offers swiftness of movement and a control of your mind which will benefit you not only when you are involved in fencing but also in everyday situations at home and in work.

Kendo does not require the great amount of training which is called for in other martial arts. Right from the start, the kendo student will be involved in the excitement of fighting with all kinds of opponents, ranging from those who are highly skilled to fellow students who are just beginning to learn the techniques.

At the outset of training, the new student of kendo learns and practises the basic techniques such as the different cuts, thrusts, slicing movements and parries shown in the following pictures. These techniques must be repeated many times to enable the fencer to gain physical and mental co-ordination as well as balance and sureness and grace of movement.

Before the outset of a training session, the fencer must loosen up by means of calisthenic exercises such as stretching (to afford suppleness), jumping (to increase leg strength) and skipping (for co-ordination).

On completion of the initial exercises the fencers normally train without full armour, practising the various techniques and movements by cutting the air time and time again. After this the fencers learn new tactical blocking and striking manoeuvres which can be experimented with in free training (keiko).

Having finished the basic training exercises and the instruction period, the fencers then dress in full armour. At this stage they face each other, the senior members (yudansha) on one side and the junior students on the other. A formal bow indicates mutual respect and is part of the kendo etiquette.

The fencers involve themselves in kirikaeshi which is a repetition of cuts and parries; one side attacks forward while the other side blocks the attacks as they move backwards. The process is then reversed. The correct form of kendo movement is also practised in kirikaeshi. The kendo step is similar to a skip. The right foot moves forward a few feet and the left foot is moved only a few inches. The rear leg then pushes forward again as the front leg steps out. This gives a spring-like action. If one foot passes the other, as in walking, this is termed a pace.

After kirikaeshi the most enjoyable part of kendo arrives. This is free training (keiko) where opponents of different stature and skill face each other in an actual combat situation. Both attack, parry and feint to find an opening to strike at. Speed and agility of mind and body as well as flexibility combined with instant reactions are necessary to be successful in fighting. It is very important for the fencers to change partners as often as possible to give the individual many opponents of varying degrees of height, build and skill. This will enable him to gain a variety of experience.

At some stage in a fencer's career whether in the practice hall (dojo) or in a competition he will be called upon to enter a shiai. This is a strictly controlled dual of two fencers who endeavour to strike and score winning cuts on each other while under the observation of referees and judges. This differs from keiko (free training) in that no experimentation or chance techniques can be risked lest a point be lost. Alertness (zanshin) must be heeded at all times as a moment of relaxation or loss of concentration could end the contest.

As in most other martial arts, kiai (shouting) is used to aid training and fencing. This is made by exploding air from the stomach and mouth as opposed to shouting from the throat. The names of the part of the armour about to be struck are usually shouted out. This indicates confidence in ability as well as complete mental and physical reaction and co-ordination.

To start training in kendo all that you require by way of equipment is a suit of armour and a bamboo sword, called a shinai. These can be bought at any martial arts shop. Your local sports shop could probably arrange to get this equipment for you.

Kendo is an excellent means of keeping your body fit and in trim as well as being one of the most effective forms of mental training. At the same time you can gain much enjoyment and friendship with others who are interested in this ancient but extremely vital sport.

The two pictures below illustrate another cut to the head. This technique can be used to hit either side of the head armour. The picture immediately below shows the shinai about to be snapped from behind the head. The bottom picture depicts the finished movement. Notice that the right hand remains in the central position as the left hand guides and controls the direction of the sword's cut.

The top picture shows a fencer lifting the shinai (bamboo sword) in preparation for a centre head cut (shomen). The picture immediately above depicts the actual striking position. The sword is guided over the head by the right hand. The left hand gives power to the cut.

The picture on the left shows a straight wrist cut. The model on the right pushes through with an effective slicing action and scores a point against his opponent. The picture on the right depicts another form of wrist cut (kote). This cut can only be effected when an opponent raises the shinai above his head and thus exposes his left wrist. Otherwise his left hand is mostly protected, being held close to the body.

This is the only sword thrust used in kendo. It is directed at the throat flap attached to the bottom front part of the head armour. Against a skilled opponent it is a very hard thrust to execute because of the speed and agility with which he can parry attacks especially if they involve a lunging action as shown in this movement. Once in this position a relatively inexperienced opponent can be manipulated.

This picture shows the opponent on the right striking his opponent's head shield with a single-handed cut. The single-handed cut is an effective way of catching an opponent by surprise and scoring a point. With practice, the single-handed cut to all parts of the body can be used with great effectiveness and skill. It must be used very quickly, however, to avoid being placed in a vulnerable position.

If both fencers score simultaneously as depicted in the picture immediately above it is called an 'Ai-auchi'. The opponent on the left effects a cut to the head. This is countered by the opponent on the right with a strike to the right side of the breast-plate (do).

There are three 'safe' positions in kendo from which opponents cannot score points. The first is the chudan no kamae where the sword is pointed at the opponent's throat to prevent an attack. The second is shown above. The third is when both fencers are out of range.

The picture on the left shows the technique necessary to block a cut to the side of the head. The sword is held vertically and pushed to either side of the body depending on the direction of attack. The picture on the right depicts the application of this block against an attack to the side of the head. This block looks very simple but in an actual combat situation must be carried out with great speed.

The picture on the left shows another kind of block against an attack to the head. The opponent on the left, moving with rapid speed, attempts a cut to the centre of the head. With equal rapidity the opponent on the right draws his sword upwards and places it across his head armour to parry the attack and prevent a point being scored.

The picture immediately above depicts a basic block. This is done by flipping the sword over to the side in a vertical position and thus covering the breastplates area. There are many ways of blocking used in kendo fighting which can be taught to you at a club.

The Art of Kendo-3

Kata, a series of stylized movements, were the main exercises performed by the ancient samurai to perfect their individual flair and technique at swordsmanship before the introduction of the bamboo sword and armour. Today the student of kendo must also learn kata during his basic training.

Kata, when performed by expert exponents, are a thrilling and spectacular display of skilled swordsmanship. This is by no means the main object of these movements, however. These exercises also develop oneness with the sword and emphasis is placed upon complete control, perfect co-ordination of movement, exact judgement of distance, absolute faultless timing and total undivided concentration. You will gain these qualities through the performance of kata as well as enjoying the physical and mental release of kendo combat.

The techniques of kata are carried out by two exponents. Each performs an exact sequence of movements in co-ordination with the other. Various attack, defence and counter attack sequences are carried out by the fencers throughout a kata. One exponent adopts the role of attacker (uchi-tachi), the other of counter attacker (shi-tachi). Although the starting and finishing actions, such as the formal salute and the drawing and sheathing of the sword, are performed slowly, the actual attacks and counters are made at full speed, the sword blade stopping just short of contact.

At the outset of kata training, the student learns the various attack and counter movements, perfecting their application by using wooden swords (bokuto). Only when the experienced student has studied and practised attacking and counter attacking roles, rehearsing these hundreds of times, will he be allowed to perform the kata with a sharp sword.

The illustrations which follow show the first sequence from the katano no kata. This is one of the most beautiful of kata and you can enjoy it by using any improvized sword such as a broom handle.

Kata are just one aspect of the exciting sport of kendo sword fighting. They are not only delightful to watch but are also invaluable ways of teaching mental and physical co-ordination. You too can learn to perform these exquisite skills by joining a kendo school.

The kata begins when both fencers face each other at a distance of 12 yards. They carry their sheathed swords in their hands. They then bow and place the swords through the left side of their body sashes. They come forward, moving the right foot first, and salute again before drawing swords.

HOW TO PLAY

Kendo probably keeps closer to the concept of martial arts than judo, karate, or aikido. The ceremonies are strictly observed before and after practice, and many kendoka (kendo exponents) have a keen interest in Japanese swords. The samurai's one aim was to destroy his opponent, so defense for its own sake was never considered. In kendo, parries are invariably followed by an immediate riposte. Every blow is accompanied by a kiai (shout), which helps tense every muscle in the body for the moment of impact. The vulnerable parts of the body are the top of the head, the sides of the body, the wrists, and the throat. All are attacked by kiri (cuts) except the throat, for which a tsuki (thrust) is used.

Footwork is vital. Short, fast gliding steps are taken, but for counter-attacking a jump is sometimes used. Tremendous emphasis is placed on the perfecting of the cut at the head – the basic attack – and most training sessions are preceded by this. Free practice with each kendoka trying to score a hit is vigorous and tiring. Training is aimed at acquiring three main qualities – skill, agility and opportunism.

The picture above depicts the execution of a shomen, a cut to the head delivered from above. Of all the kendo cuts (kiri) this is one of the most highly regarded. In the age of the samurai the helmets worn were composed of two pieces and joined at the crown. A cut to the head could thus prove fatal.

The fencers then stand up and adopt the chudan no kamae stance, the basic fighting position of kendo. The right foot is placed forward and the sword is symbolically aimed at the throat of the opponent.

The above picture shows the second movement of the kata. Both fencers squat, holding the handle of the sword in the right hand. They remain in this position for a period of a few seconds to aid concentration.

Both swords are then drawn as depicted immediately above. The fencers cross blades and again pause as part of the etiquette which is involved in kendo. This signifies respect between the opponents.

The two pictures immediately above show the two fencers tilting their swords to the right. The fencers then move back five short paces and once again adopt the fighting stance depicted in the lower picture.

The large picture below depicts the beginning of the action. The attacker (uchi-tachi) adopts the jodan no kamae stance, moving his left foot forward and raising his sword over his head.

The above picture shows the counter attacker (shi-tachi) adopt the jodan no kamae stance. But his right foot remains in the forward position.

Both fencers glide forward three paces. The attacker moves the left foot first, the counter attacker moves the right foot first.

The attacker then begins a head cut (shomen). The counter attacker avoids this by stepping back one move with his left foot.

The Samurai Sword

It is extremely difficult to know where the first samurai swords used in Japan were made. The few swords that have been found have not been tempered and the majority are of the straight variety.

It is thought, however, that immigrants from Mongolia brought single-edged, pointed iron swords to Japan around the second century. It was not until the seventh century that the traditional curved blade first appeared. Legend ascribes its introduction to the swordsmith Amakuni.

One day Amakuni and his son watched the warriors returning from battle. Amakuni was the head swordsmith and it was traditional that he should be given a signal of recognition from the emperor as he led his troops back from war. The emperor passed him by, completely ignoring him.

At first Amakuni was puzzled but then noticed that most of the returning warriors were carrying broken swords. After gathering these swords, Amakuni examined them thoroughly and found that they were not tempered correctly. Remembering the emperor's rebuff he decided to forge the perfect sword. He worked relentlessly with his subordinate swordsmiths.

At the end of one long month they appeared with a sword with a curved blade. The warriors laughed at him but Amakuni polished and ground his sword to razor sharpness. In the spring the emperor left with his warriors to fight in another war, taking the new swords which Amakuni had made. Several months passed. One morning Amakuni heard the samurai returning. He ran to the door and counted the blades. None were broken. As the emperor passed he turned to Amakuni and said, 'You are truly a great swordsmith.' Amakuni rejoiced.

The counter attacker scores a cut to the head by moving one pace forward with the right foot. He symbolically places his sword just above the attacker's head. The attacker acknowledges the cut stopping his sword in the gedan no kamae position, pointing towards the knees of his opponent.

The counter attacker, on the left, then moves back one pace as shown in the above picture. He raises his sword over his head and adopts the jodan no kamae stance. This whole position is called a zanshin (alertness) stance. The attacker, on the right, remains in the same position, sword held downwards.

The picture immediately above depicts the conclusion of the kata sequence. The counter attacker lowers his sword, the attacker raises his sword and both fencers then cross blades as at the beginning.

The fencers then tilt their swords once again. They then move five short paces backward adopt the chudan no kamae stance, move three paces forward, cross swords and squat. After this they replace the swords in their sheaths, stand up, bow to each other and move five short paces backward. They finish with a final bow before removing the sheathed swords from the body sashes with the right hand.

The Art of Kendo—4

The origin of the samurai warrior was due to the numerous hostile clans which had settled throughout medieval Japan. Because of constant fighting, a warrior of no mean ability developed. The samurai was the central figure of this era, an aristocratic fighting man renowned for his skill. as a horseman, archer and swordsman. Such skills were used either to defend his own lands or to aid those to whom he owed allegiance, his clan chief or even the emperor himself. In many respects the samurai can be compared to the knight of feudal England who, in exchange for lands, fought for his king. They were both accomplished horsemen and studied the many weapons available in their respective cultures.

Although in modern times the samurai is depicted as a swordsman, the earlier Japanese warrior only boasted of his skill with the bow and usually played down his ability with the sword. It was not until a 13th-century edict banned the wearing of swords that the long, single-edged, two-handed sword became the symbol of the warrior, displacing the bow as the chief weapon. This was because the samurai and court nobles were the only people allowed to use swords. In this sense the sword came to represent superiority and fear.

About this time a new philosophy was introduced into Japan by Buddhist monks returning from China. This was called zen (meaning meditation) and rapidly spread throughout Japan. Because of its inherent austerity the many samurai of the time sought to learn its perfections. The majority of the samurai mastered the meaning of zen and in their later years usually adopted a religious life.

The aim of zen is to gain complete control of the mind in order to attain a state of enlightenment and a sense of detachment from the physical world. This is achieved by constant meditation and strict self-discipline. Zen enhances the character and well-being of any person who strives to achieve its perfections.

The samurai realized the power of zen and used the control it gave him even when fighting. His studies in this philosophy and his immense skill with all kinds of weapons enabled him to hold a feared but honoured place in Japanese society. The remnants of this still exist in modern Japan.

The advent of modern weaponry caused the redundancy of the sword as an effective weapon on the battlefield. Instead, sword-fighting techniques and the whole philosophy of the samurai became a form of sport and a means to discipline the mind and body. This non-fighting way of the sword became known as kendo.

Kendo is an excellent means by which you can achieve physical agility and prowess as well as complete control of your mental faculties. And this can be done while you are enjoying yourself.

Kendo involves all the techniques of samurai fencing using a specially designed bamboo sword called the shinai. This sword and the simple armour worn in practice enables you to fight with full vigour and strength without causing any injuries. The result is an exhilarating form of physical release by which you can unleash many of the stresses and strains with which you have to cope in everyday life. As you become, more skilled in the techniques of using the shinai you can then progress to learning the mental discipline which kendo teaches.

The pictures which follow show you some more aspects of kendo sword fighting. The art of drawing a sword with maximum skill and advantage is depicted. So also is the use of other martial arts, such as karate, as combined with fencing techniques. Both of these subjects are practised by kendo students who have already achieved a certain amount of proficiency in the use of the sword. They will give you an idea, however, of some of the more exciting aspects of kendo to which you can progress when you have mastered the basics. They are techniques to which you can look forward. But even at the beginning of a kendo course you will enjoy the excitement of fighting with bamboo swords without fear of hurting yourself or your opponents. You can start combat almost immediately on joining a club.

Kendo offers you a way of achieving both physical and mental fitness in a colourful, exhilarating and totally engrossing way.

The samurai were complete fighters and used the skills of other martial arts besides sword fighting. The large picture on the right shows a head kick during a fight. The insert pictures depict one of the techniques of EI-AI, the art of drawing the sword. A quick and skilful draw could create an early advantage which could be decisive.
The samurai spent many long hours learning to withdraw, strike and replace the sword with lightning speed. Slowness of withdrawal could cancel excellent technique.

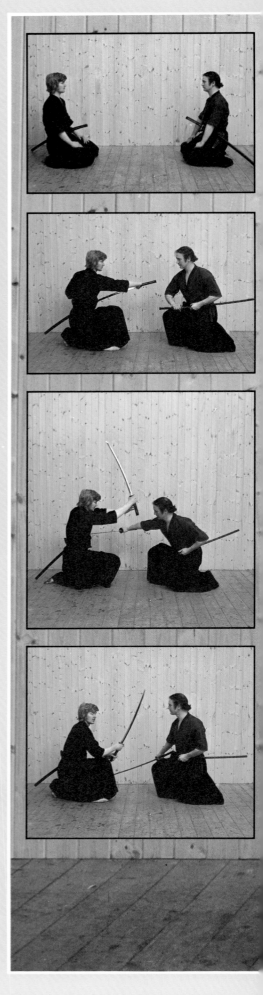

At close quarters the samurai frequently used hand-fighting techniques both to gain advantage or if he was rendered weaponless. All of these techniques were carried out at a very fast pace. The skilful warrior was adept at a number of martial arts and could use these in any situation on the battlefield.

The three pictures above illustrate another EI-AI technique. In this case it is combined with a karate kick. The fencer on the left pretends to draw his sword. Having tricked his opponent by not drawing, he executes an effective kick to the head. He would then follow this with a sword cut.

The Samurai Armour

The armour worn by the samurai originated from different parts of Asia and was improved and added to by the Japanese who eventually produced a suit of several thousand pieces. Only the wealthy could usually afford such armour. The ordinary soldier wore only what he had been given, which was sometimes augmented by extra pieces he collected on the battlefields. The samuari armour was much lighter and flexible than that worn by the European knights of the same period. The armour was made from bamboo and jade worked into a beautiful and ornate suit which served as an extremely effective form of protection from sword blows and the raining arrows of the enemy. Because of this each samurai trained at hitting the most vulnerable parts of the armour —where the different pieces were joined. To do this required hard and persistent slashes. The helmet, for example, was usually joined in the middle. Two fighting samurai warriors would try to smash each other's helmet so as to gain an important opening.
A simple form of armour is worn in kendo practice sessions to allow full physical release without danger of hurt.

The above three pictures show another example of an EI-AI technique. The insert picture depicts the opponents facing each other. The fencer on the right tricks his opponent by hitting him in the groin with the handle of the sword. This breaks his opponent's concentration, allowing the fencer to complete an effective slicing cut to the neck.